# OLKESTONE - DOVI

## EAL · HYTHE · NEW ROMNEY

C000246456

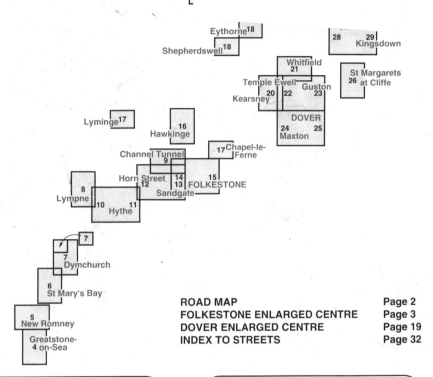

| | |
|---|---|
| ROAD MAP | Page 2 |
| FOLKESTONE ENLARGED CENTRE | Page 3 |
| DOVER ENLARGED CENTRE | Page 19 |
| INDEX TO STREETS | Page 32 |

Every effort has been made to verify the accuracy of information in this book but the publishers cannot accept responsibility for expense or loss caused by an error or omission. Information that will be of assistance to the user of the maps will be welcomed.

The representation on these maps of a road, track or path is no evidence of the existence of a right of way.

| | |
|---|---|
| Car Park | P |
| Public Convenience | C |
| Place of Worship | + |
| One-way Street | → |
| Pedestrianized | ▨ |
| Post Office | ● |

**Scale of street plans 4 inches to 1 mile**
**Unless otherwise stated**

Street plans prepared and published by ESTATE PUBLICATIONS, Bridewell House, TENTERDEN, KENT, and based upon the ORDNANCE SURVEY mapping with the permission of The Controller of H. M. Stationery Office.

The Publishers acknowledge the co-operation of the local authorities of towns represented in this atlas.

state Publications 028 M          ISBN 1 84192 059 2          © Crown Copyright 398713

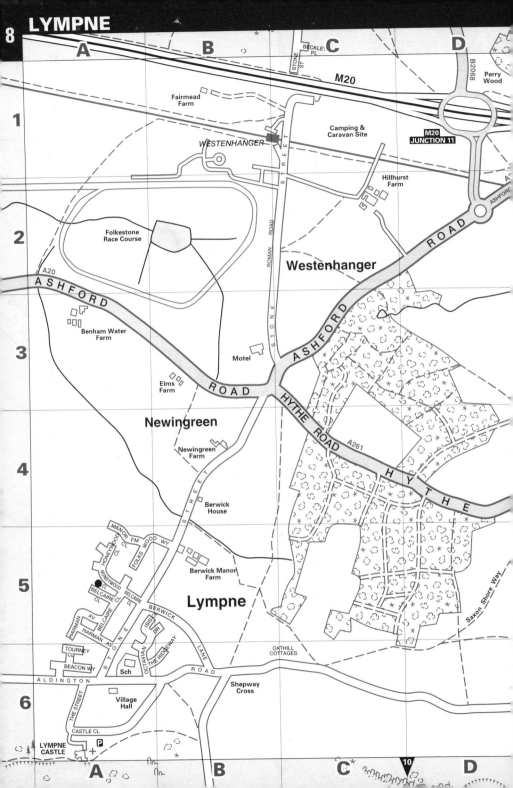

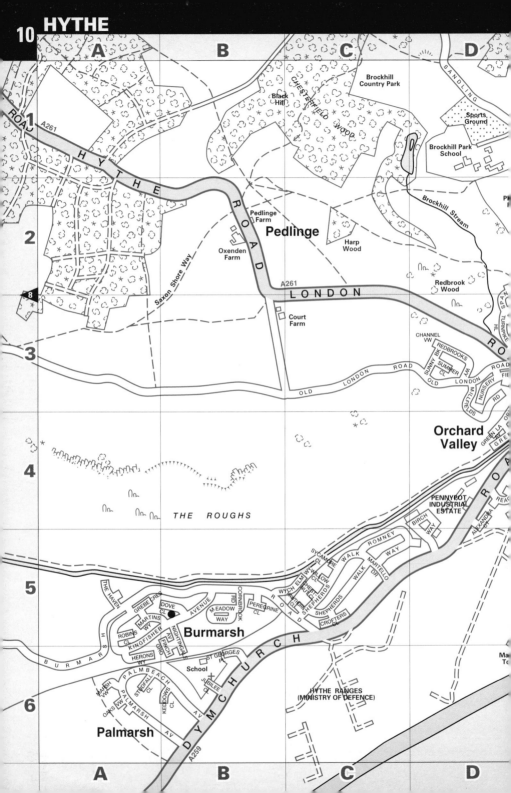

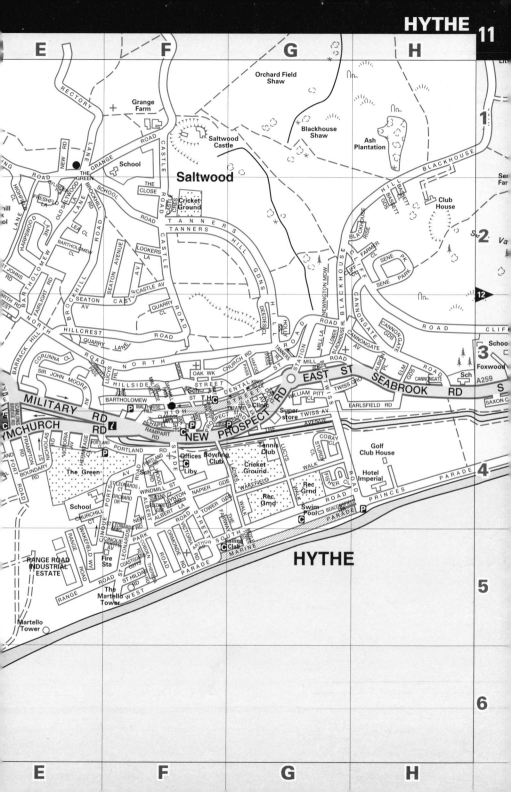

E   F   G   H

Orchard Field
Shaw

Grange
Farm

RECTORY LANE

GRANGE ROAD

NEW RD

THE GREEN

School

Saltwood
Castle

Blackhouse
Shaw

Ash
Plantation

BLACKHOUSE

Saltwood

THE CLOSE

CASTLE ROAD

SCHOOL ROAD

Cricket
Ground

TANNERS

TANNERS

HILL GDNS

CLUB HOUSE

HILL RISE

BASSETT GDS

Club
House

SENE PK

SENE PARK

FRESHFLD CL

HIGHFLD CL

OLD SALTWOOD LANE

LEA CL

BROCKHILL RD

BARTHOLOMEW CL

LOOKERS LA

CASTLE AV

SEATON AVENUE

QUARRY CL

CASTLE ROAD

BLACKHOUSE HILL

CANNONGATE

CLIFF RD

FARMER CL

CANNONGATE GDS

SENE

CANNONGATE AV

ROAD

12

HARPSWOOD LANE

ST JOHNS RD

BARTHOLOMEW LA

SEATON AV

HILLCREST

QUARRY LANE

NORTH

DEEDES CL

HILL

LOWER BLACKHOUSE HILL

CANNONGATE

ROAD

ALBIN PL

ELM GDS

CANNONGATE

ROAD

A259

School

Foxwood

Sch

BARRACK HILL

NORTH RD

CORUNNA CL

SIR JOHN MOORE AV

LUCYS HL

HILLSIDE

OAK WK

CHURCH RD

STREET

Sch

St

T.H.C.

HIGH ST

DENTAL

SWN CL

KINGS

STATION ROAD

MILL LA

MILL

TWISS GRO

SEABROOK RD

SAXON CL

MILITARY RD

SCANLONS BRIDGE RD

BARTHOLOMEW

MALTHOUSE

CHAPEL ST

CLARKS

RAMPART RD

PROSPECT RD

THEATRE ST

Clinic

WILLIAM PITT

TWISS RD

EARLSFIELD RD

Super-
store

TWISS AV

NEW PROSPECT

EAST ST

YMCHURCH RD

FRAMPTON RD

VICTORIA RD

NICHOLAS

HERMITAGE

PORTLAND

PORTLAND AV

Sch

COBAY CL

LUCYS

STURDY

AVENUE

Tennis
Club

Offices

Bowling
Club

Liby

Cricket
Ground

LADIES

WAKEFIELD

WALK

WALK

Rec
Grnd

Golf
Club House

Hotel
Imperial

PARADE

FISHER CL

PRINCES ROAD

4

AND FORT ROAD

BOUNDARY RD

The Green

CHURCHILL CT

School

ST LEONARDS CT

ORCHARD DR

WINDMILL ST

NAPIER GDS

Sch

QUEENS RD

ALBERT LA

ALBERT

TOWER GDS

Rec
Grnd

Swim
Pool

BEACONSFIELD

CINQUE PORTS ST

ST LEONARDS RD

NEW RD

VICTORIA RD

ARTHUR RD

SOUTH FAIRWAY

THE WALK

Sailing
Club

MARINE PARADE

HYTHE

RANGE ROAD
INDUSTRIAL
ESTATE

WAKEFIELD WY

RANGE ROAD

CINQUE AV

ST LEONARDS PARK

COBDEN RD

ORMONDE RD

COASTGUARDS COTTS

RANGE RD

Fire
Sta

The
Martello
Tower

ST HILDAS RD

WEST PARADE

Martello
Tower

E   F   G   H

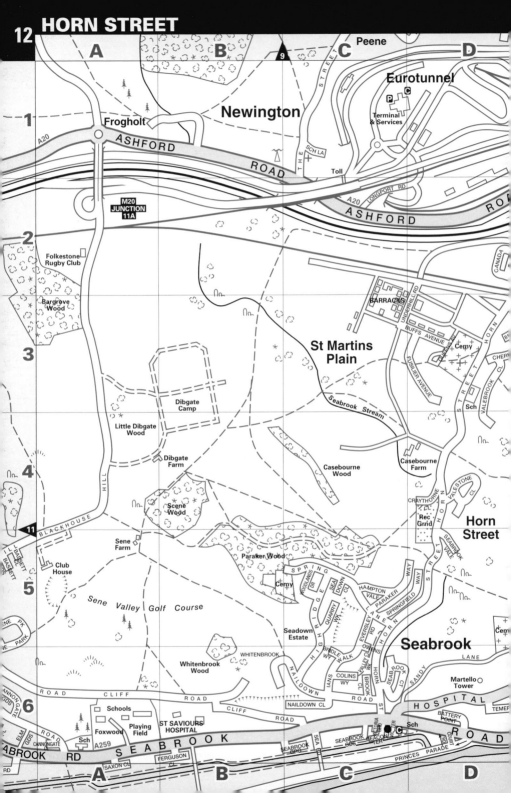

Peene

A      B      C      D

**Eurotunnel**

Terminal & Services

Toll

**Newington**

Frogholt

ASHFORD   ROAD

THE STREET

LONGPORT RD

A20

A20   ASHFORD   RD

M20 JUNCTION 11A

Folkestone Rugby Club

CANADA

BARRACKS

Bargrove Wood

UNDERHILL RD

BUFFS AVENUE

Cemy

HORN STREET

CHERI

**St Martins Plain**

FUSILIER AVENUE

VALEBROOK CL

Dibgate Camp

Sch

Little Dibgate Wood

Seabrook   Stream

Dibgate Farm

Casebourne Wood

Casebourne Farm

Scene Wood

CRAYTHORNE

VALESTONE CL

HILL

**Horn Street**

Rec Grnd

BLACKHOUSE

HORN STREET

SEABROOK VALE

Sene Farm

Club House

Paraken Wood

SPRING

Cemy

WOODLANDS DR

SEA DOWN CL

HAMPTON VALE

PARAKER WAY

SPRINGFIELD WAY

WAY

HORN STREET

BASSETT

BASSETT

**Seabrook**

Sene Valley Golf Course

HIGH RIDGE

QUARRY WAY

BRIDLE WAY

EVERSLEY RD

OWENS CL

Seadown Estate

WHITENBROOK

IANS WY

COLINS WY

NAILDOWN

VALLEY RD

HORN BROOK

SEAB CK CL

LANE

SANDY

Martello Tower

Whitenbrook Wood

Cemy

ROAD   CLIFF

ROAD

CLIFF   ROAD

NAILDOWN CL

ST

ROAD

HOSPITAL   ROAD

BATTERY POINT

TEMPE

Schools

CANNON GATE

ELMS GDS

CANNINGATE ROAD

Foxwood

Sch

Playing Field

ST SAVIOURS HOSPITAL

SEABROOK

SAXON CL

FERGUSON CL

A259   SEABROOK

SEABROOK BDGE

SEABROOK

SEABROOK GDS

BEACONSFIELD TER

VICTORIA RD

Sch

COURT RD

PRINCES PARADE

A      B      C      D

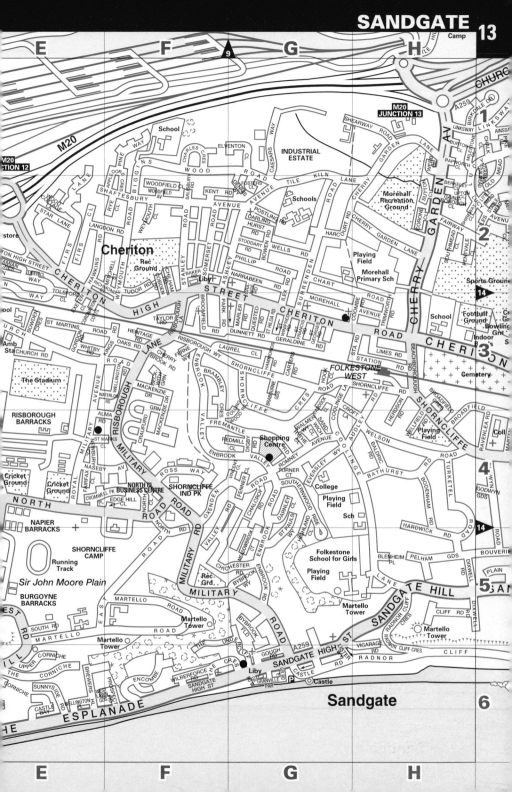

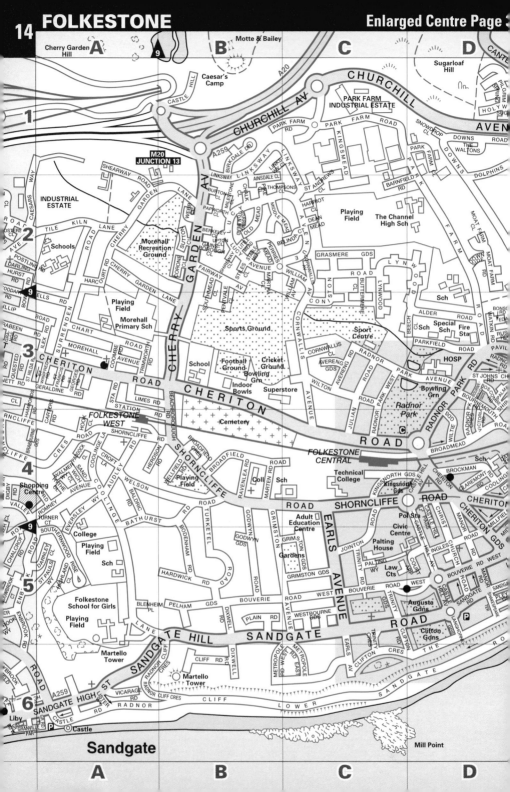

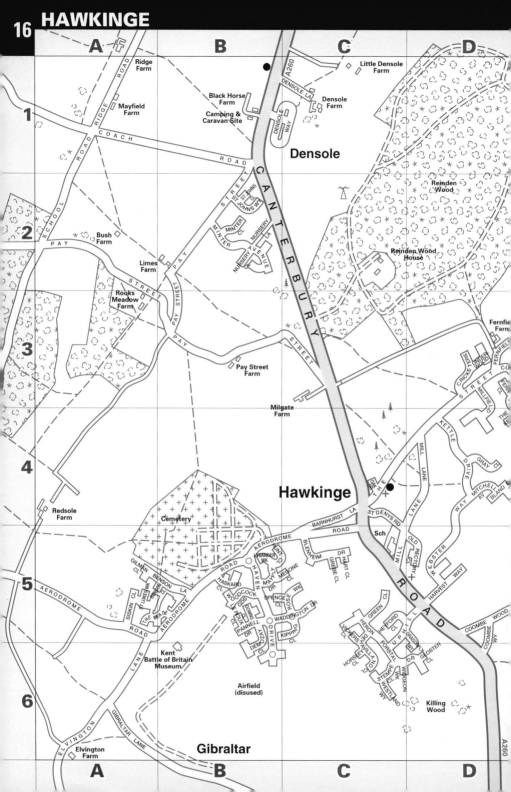

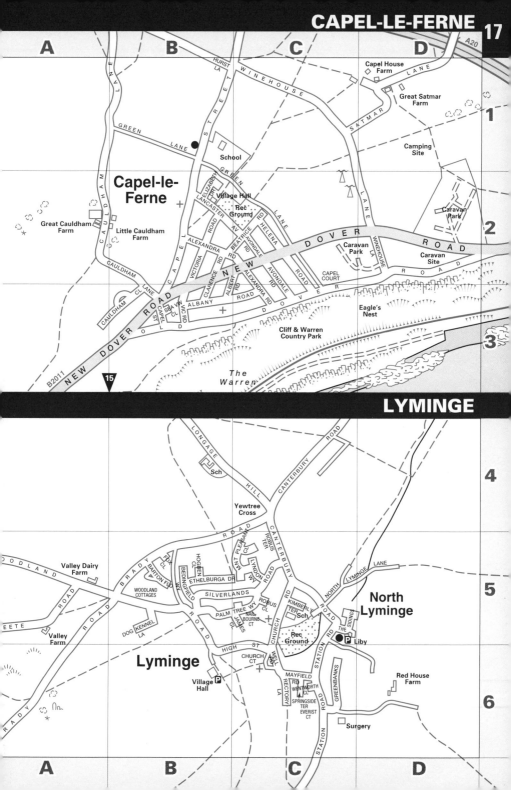

A20

**A**    **B**    **C**    **D**

HURST LA

WINEHOUSE

Capel House Farm

Great Satmar Farm

GREEN LANE

STREET

SATMAR LANE

**1**

School

Camping Site

GREEN LANE

## Capel-le-Ferne

ELIZABETH

Village Hall

Rec Ground

HELENA RD

Caravan Park

**2**

Great Cauldham Farm

Little Cauldham Farm

LANCASTER AV

BEATRICE RD

AVONDALE

WINEHOUSE LA

Caravan Park

ALEXANDRA

VICTORIA RD

NEW

AVONDALE RD

DOVER

Caravan Site

CAULDHAM

CLARENCE RD

ALEXANDRA ROAD

ROAD

CAPEL COURT

ROAD

CAULDHAM LANE

CAPEL

SEA VW CL

ALBERT RD

ALBANY

DOVER

Eagle's Nest

**3**

NEW DOVER ROAD

VIC RD

CL

Cliff & Warren Country Park

B2011

**15**

*The Warren*

---

LONGAGE ROAD

CANTERBURY ROAD

Sch

**4**

HILL ROAD

Yewtree Cross

CANTERBURY ROAD

NORTH LYMINGE LANE

WOODLAND ROAD

Valley Dairy Farm

BRADY RD

BARTON FLD WY

HOGBEN CL

MNT PLEASANT

ROBUS TER

LYNDON WY

ETHELBURGA DR

**North Lyminge**

**5**

EETE

BEDINGFIELD

SILVERLANDS

KIMBERL TER

Sch

THE SIDING

Liby

Valley Farm

DOG KENNEL LA

PALM TREE WY

ROBUS CL

NAIL BOURNE CT

CHURCH ROAD

STATION RD

WOODLAND COTTAGES

JAMES

Rec Ground

Red House Farm

**Lyminge**

HIGH ST

WELL

GREENBANKS

Village Hall

CHURCH CT

RECTORY

MAYFIELD RD

WENTWORTH CL

SPRINGSIDE TER

EVEREST CT

Surgery

**6**

BRADY

**A**    **B**    **C**    **D**

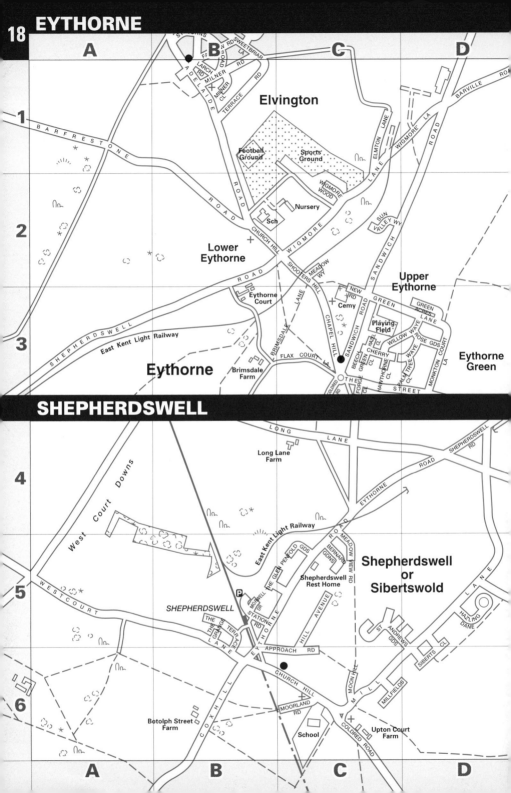

A B C D

# EYTHORNE

Elvington

Football Ground

Sports Ground

WIGMORE WOOD

Nursery

Sch

Lower Eythorne

CHURCH HILL

WIGMORE

SHOOTERS HILL

MEADOW WY

SUN

VALLEY WY

SANDWICH

Upper Eythorne

NEW RD

Cemy

GREEN

GREEN LA

Playing Field

SANDWICH ROAD

BEECH

GREEN CHERRY

FORGE

HAWTHORNE

CL

WILLOW WAYE

PALM TREE WAYE

ROSE GDNS

MONKTON CT

Eythorne Green

Eythorne Court

BRIMSDALE LANE

CHAPEL HILL

FLAX COURT

Eythorne

Brimsdale Farm

THE GREEN

STREET

COLDRED RD

SHEPHERDSWELL

East Kent Light Railway

BARFRESTONE

ROAD

ROAD

ELMTON LANE

WIGMORE LA

BARVILLE RD

ROAD

# SHEPHERDSWELL

LONG LANE

Long Lane Farm

West Court Downs

East Kent Light Railway

SHEPHERDSWELL RD

EYTHORNE ROAD

Shepherdswell or Sibertswold

MEADOW VIEW RD

BERNARD GDNS

PENFOLD GDNS

THE GLEN

Shepherdswell Rest Home

SHEPHERDSWELL

P

MILL WELL DR

STATION RD

THE TERRACE

FITCH LANE

AVENUE

HILL

ST ANDREWS GDNS

HAZLING DANE

SIBERTS CL

WESTCOURT

APPROACH RD

MOON HILL

M I L L LANE

MILLFIELDS

CROOKHILL RD

CHURCH HILL

MOORLAND RD

Botolph Street Farm

School

COLDRED ROAD

Upton Court Farm

A B C D

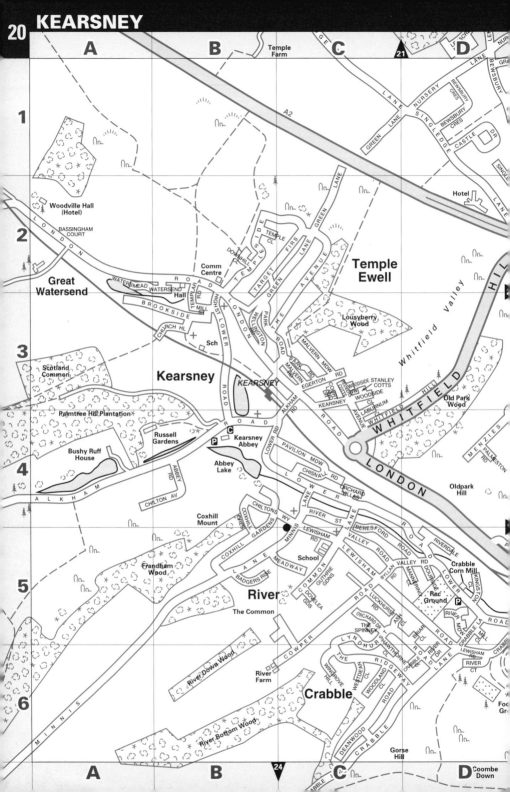

Little Pineham Farm

Great Pineham Farm

PINEHAM ROAD

23 PINEHAM

North Downs Way & White Cliffs Country Trail

WHITFIELD - EASTRY BY - PASS

JUBILEE WAY

Light Hill

Barntye Shaw

WHITFIELD ROAD

Parsonage Farm

COURT

F

E

DURBAN

WYCHERLEY AVENUE

23

e Path

School

MELBOURNE AVENUE

Whitfield

DRIVE

BURGESS DOWNSLEIGH CL

FARNCOMBE CL

COX WOOD CL

CRANLEIGH

BEAUXFIELD

CRANLEIGH DR

ALLISON

NACHESTER

MILL

THE DROVE

CHAPEL RD

FORGE AVENUE

CHESTNUT CL

GUILFORD

NURSERY LA

GRACE

LENACRE LA

THE PIER

ORCHARD

FLOUR

LENACRE AV

THE ACRE

Lenacre Farm

Lenacre Wood

NURSERY LANE

SINGLEDGE LANE

GREEN LANE

Temple Farm

SINGLEDGE

A2

NEWLANDS

NEWLANDS

NEWLANDS AV

COURTLAND

JOYES CL

JOYES RD

CRES

School

MAYFIELD ROAD

ALLISON CL

MANLEY CL

MAYFIELD RD

Fire Sta

ARCHERS

SANDWICH

ROAD

MDW

BEWSBURY CROSS LANE

SINGLEDGE AV

BEWSBURY CRES

BEWSBURY CRES

CASTLE DR

CASTLE

Hotel

Superstores

Council Offices

WHITFIELD CT

WHITE CLIFFS BUSINESS PARK

JUBILEE

PARKWAY

HONEYWOOD

Playing Field

HONEYWOOD

HONEYWOOD RD

HONEYWOOD

MARY GDN

BLEKO GORDON BOSON

RD

HENNIKER CL

FRANCE RD

WELLINGTON RD

RD

KEDELSTON RD

OLD PARK

OLD PARK

School

MELBOURNE RD

FULBERT RD

HIRST CL

ROKESLEY

COLLINGWOOD RD

WOTHERLEY

HIRST CL

BRASSEY

C

D

22

S21

Whitfield Valley

Old Park Wood

WHITFIELD HILL

Temple Ewell

Lousberry Wood

Old Park Wood

WOODSIDE STANLEY COTTS

WOODBINE

CORNUM

KEARSNEY

MALVERN MDW

MALVERN RD

PARK

WELLINGTON PARK

FIRS

TEMPLE GREEN

TARGET GREEN LANE

AVENUE

MALVERN ROAD

EGERTON RD

KEARSNEY AVENUE

STANLEY RD

GRANUM

URBURN RD

ALKHAM RD

KRSNEY

A

B

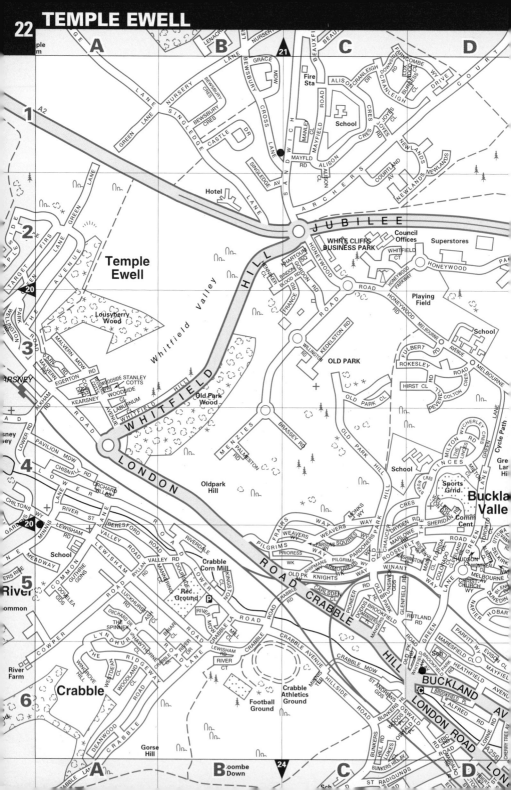

E F 21 G iffords overt H

Light
Hill

North Downs Way & White Cliffs Country Trail

PINEHAM ROAD

PINEHAM ROAD

LANGDON ROAD

Gustoncourt
Farm

EASTRY BY-PASS

WAY

JUBILEE

A2

THE STREET

THE CHANGE

BARNTYE VILLAS

BROMPTON CL

MDW

PRESCOTT CL

LANE

HANGMANS LANE

**Guston**

BRICKFIELD
COTTAGES

Barntye
Shaw

1

2

3

Frith
Farm

ST MARTINS RD

DOVER ROAD

WAY

A258 DEAL RD

URBAN CRES

NATAL RD

TENNYSON BLDGS

URBAN CL

KIMBERLEY CL

ROMAN ROAD

ROMAN ROAD

ROAD

Long
Hill

Playing
Field

The Danes
Rec Ground

DOVER ROAD

ROAD

CHARLTON

Duke of York's
Royal Military School

TANGIER

GIBRALTA SQ

DUNKIRK SQ

CORRINA

LYNE PL

HEIGHTS

LUCKNOW CL

NAMUR PL

KOHIMA PL

ALAMEIN CL

Sch

BURGOYNE

ANZIO CRES

CASSINO SQ

4

5

DEAL RD

ROAD

DOVER ROAD

Chafiton
Cemetery

DANES CT

DANES CT

ROMAN ROAD

ckland

Schools

Cemetery

Jewish
Cemy

St. Marys
Cemetery

C

URBAN AV

NATAL RD

STANHOPE RD

ASTLEY AV

BEACHSFLD

CHARLTON

TINGLE AV

ON ROAD

CONNAUGHT

CASTLE

ALFRED

Fort
Burgoyne

Connaught
Barracks

SOUTH FORELAND

DEAL RD

JUBILEE

WAY

A258

A2

6

E F 25 G RD H

Connau ht
Park

St Radigunds

Tower Hamlets

Elms Vale

Maxton

Aycliff

Little Farthingloe

Great Farthingloe

Coney Hill

Elms Wood

Recreation Ground

Buckland Hospital

BUCKLAND HOSPITAL

HOLMESTONE RD IND EST

POULTON CL BUSINESS PK

COOMBE VALLEY INDUSTRIAL ESTATE

H.M. Young Offenders Institution

Round Down

Shakespeare Tunnel

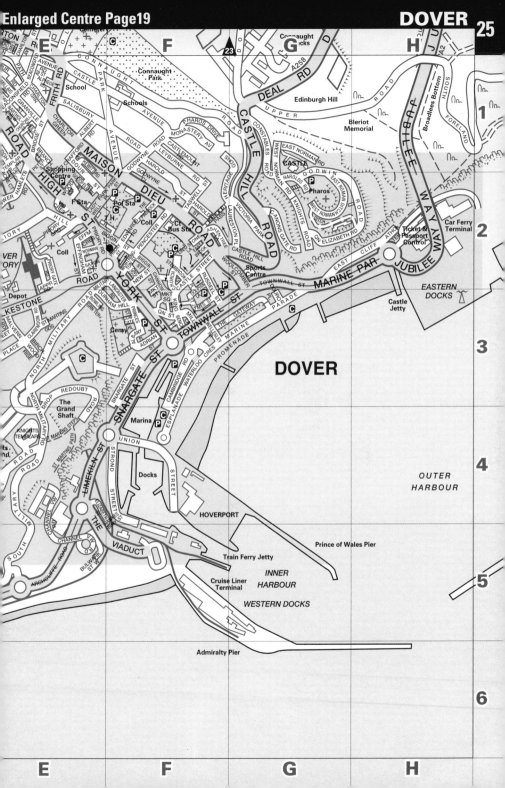

E F G H

1

2

3

4

5

6

E F G H

**DOVER**

**OUTER HARBOUR**

**INNER HARBOUR**

**WESTERN DOCKS**

Admiralty Pier

Prince of Wales Pier

Cruise Liner Terminal

Train Ferry Jetty

HOVERPORT

Docks

Marina

The Grand Shaft

KNIGHTS TEMPLARS

REDOUBT

THE VIADUCT

Cemy

Depot

Coll

VER ORY

Connaught Park

School

Schools

Edinburgh Hill

Connaught Docks

Bleriot Memorial

CASTLE

Pharos

Car Ferry Terminal

Ticket & Passport Control

Castle Jetty

EASTERN DOCKS

Sports Centre

Bus Sta

Shopping Centre

Pol Sta

T.H.

Coll

Broadlees Bottom

# St Margarets at Cliffe

St Margaret
Free Down

Barrow
Mount

Old Bottom
Free Down

East Valley
Farm

Nelson

Park

Bockhill
Farm

Bockell
Hill

NELSON PARK RD
SEYMOUR RD
HARDY RD
COLLINGWOOD RD
ST VINCENT
ROAD
STATION

THE FREEDOWN
ROAD
MILLFIELD
KINGSDOWN
THE AVENUE
CHAPEL
DOVER ROAD
ROAD
Townsend
Farm
TOWNSEND
FARM RD
WELL LANE
HIGH STREET
VICTORIA RD
HEATHER
ROYSTON GDS
GEORGE PL
REACH CRES PL
GLEBE CL
ABINGDON CL
REACH
RD
REACH WAY
REACH CL
REACH MEADOW
CHURCHILL
ROMAN
SEA LANE
DROVEWAY
School
KENILWORTH
GDNS
CONVENT CL
DOWNSIDE
THE STREET
SALISBURY HILL
GRANVILLE RD
LONG HILL
DROVEWAY
THE RISE
DROMAN RD
CAVENDISH RD
HOTEL HILL
VICTORIA AV
ROAD
ROAD
The Leas

King George
Park
Hall
Fire
Sta
St Margarets
Country Club

Bay Hill

BAY HILL
BAY HILL CL
BAY HILL

ST MARGARETS
BAY

ST MARGARETS ROAD
FORELAND ROAD
LIGHTHOUSE
SEA VIEW
GOODWIN
FORELAND
CROSS RD
SEA VIEW ROAD
THE BEACH
THE CRES
THE CRESTS ROAD
THE CRES
BEACH ROAD
FRONT

Reach Court
Farm

The Pines
Garden

Mus    Ness Point

Wanstone
Farm

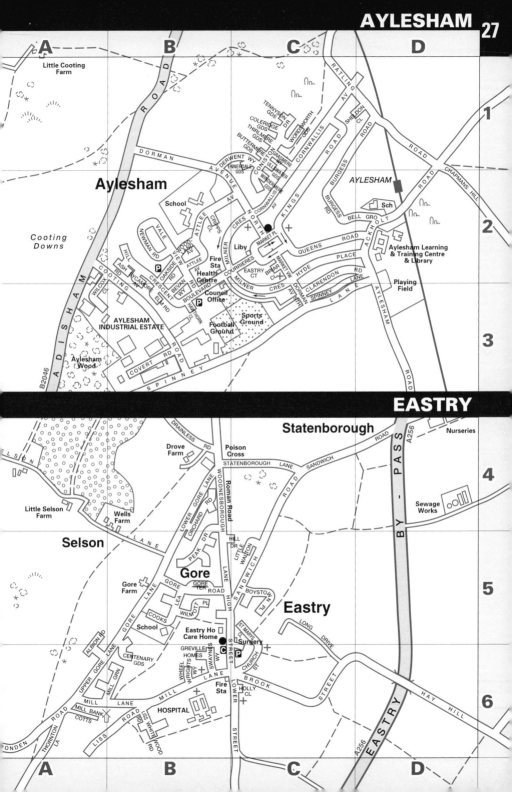

**A** **B** **C** **D**

Little Cooting Farm

R O A D

RD

D O R M A N

A V E N U E

Aylesham

Cooting Downs

School

ENNERDALE GDS

TENNYSON GDS

COLERIDGE GDS

THIRLMERE GDS

BUTTERMERE GDS

DERWENT WY

ULLSWATER

CONISTON GDS

WINDERMERE

GRASMERE

WORDSWORTH GDS

CORNWALLIS

CORNWALLIS DR

RATLING

AV

SHELDON RD

SHELDON CL

BURGESS ROAD

BURGESS RD

KINGS ROAD

BELL GRO

ACKHOLT

ROAD

CHAPMANS HILL

AYLESHAM

Sch

Aylesham Learning & Training Centre & Library

VALE

NEWMAN RD

HILL RD

ASH RD

RYCHMORE WY

CRESCENT

OAKSIDE RD

NEWTON AV

ATTLEE

BEVAN RD

ATTLEE AV

CRIPPS

MILNER

NORTH CRES

CORNWALLIS DR

MARKET PL

EASTRY CT

BRIAR

COURRIERES

MARKET VW

QUEENS ROAD

HYDE

PLACE

CLARENDON RD

LANE

Playing Field

Liby

Fire Sta

Health Centre

Council Office

Sports Ground

ELM RD

BOULEVARD

HAWTHORN

AYLESHAM INDUSTRIAL ESTATE

Football Ground

MILNER CRES

DORMAN

AV STH

SPINNEY

AYLESHAM ROAD

ROAD

COVERT

S P I N N E Y

Aylesham Wood

R O A D

B2046

A D I S H A M

COOTING

WILCOX CL

WILLOW AV

P

P

Statenborough

Nurseries

DRAINLESS RD

Drove Farm

Poison Cross

STATENBOROUGH LANE

SANDWICH

ROAD

A256

B Y - P A S S

Sewage Works

NELSON

Little Selson Farm

Wells Farm

LANE

Selson

LOWER GORE LANE

ORCHARD GORE LANE

PEAK DR

WOODNESBOROUGH

Roman Road

HILL DR

LITTLE WALTON

SANDWICH ROAD

HIGH

LANE

BOYSTOWN PL

Eastry

Gore

Gore Farm

GORE TER

GORE ROAD

LEA

WILMOT PL

COOKS

School

CENTENARY GDS

ALBION RD

UPPER GORE LANE

GORE LANE

MILL GRN

ST MARYS PL

Eastry Ho Care Home

GREVILLE HOMES

WHEELWRIGHTS WY

HAYWAYS

STREET

Surgery

CHURCH STREET

BROOK

HOLLY CL

Fire Sta

LONG DRIVE

BROOK STREET

HAY HILL

E A S T R Y

A256

HOSPITAL

MILL LANE

MILL ROAD

LISS WHITEWOOD RD

LOWER STREET

MILL BANK COTTS

THORNTON LA

LISS ROAD

ONDEN

P

C